For Fiona and Jake – J.Z.

First edition for the United States, Canada, and the Philippines published 2004
by Barron's Educational Series, Inc.

Lanterns and Firecrackers copyright © Frances Lincoln Limited 2004
Text copyright © Jonny Zucker 2004
Illustrations copyright © Jan Barger Cohen 2004

First published in Great Britain in 2004 by
Frances Lincoln Limited, 4 Torriano Mews,
Torriano Avenue, London NW5 2RZ
www.franceslincoln.com

All inquiries should be addressed to:
Barron's Educational Series, Inc.
250 Wireless Boulevard
Hauppauge, New York 11788
http://www.barronseduc.com

Library of Congress Catalog Card No.: 2003110645
ISBN-13: 978-0-7641-2668-0
ISBN-10: 0-7641-2668-7

Printed in Singapore
9 8 7 6 5 4

The Publishers would like to thank Cosima Bruno from SOAS
for checking the text and illustrations.

FESTIVAL TIME!

Lanterns and Firecrackers

A Chinese New Year Story

Jonny Zucker

Illustrated by Jan Barger Cohen

Soon it will be Chinese New Year.
We're cleaning our home
and putting flowers everywhere.

We set off firecrackers
to scare away any bad spirits
and to welcome the New Year.

It's the first day
and I'm wearing new clothes
for the new and good things
to come.

My brother and I are each given
an envelope with money inside.
The envelopes are red –
a color of luck.

Today, our family and friends
bring food and drink.
We sit down and enjoy
a great feast.

We watch the amazing
lion and dragon dances.

On the last day of the festival
we hang up the lanterns outside
and wish for good luck
in our special New Year.

What is Chinese New Year about?

Each year, on the first new moon of the lunar calendar, Chinese people start to celebrate New Year, also called Spring Festival. It is a joyful festival that starts with the new moon and ends on the full moon fifteen days later.

In all homes this is a time for family reunion. Good wishes are inscribed on slips of red paper and silk scrolls and posted up on walls and doors. Flowers, oranges, and candied fruit make colorful decorations, while fireworks are set off to frighten evil spirits away and welcome in the New Year.

On New Year's Eve a delicious banquet is prepared in honor of the family ancestors and to celebrate family unity. This event is called **weilu**, "gathering around the stove." It honors past and present generations. A whole fish is served, but some must be left over to represent prosperity for the coming year. Noodles represent long life. And dumplings signify all the good things that come wrapped in small packages!

On the night of the full moon, a great number of lanterns are hung up in houses and on streets. Made of transparent paper or thin silk, these illuminations are of varied colors and in diverse shapes, representing phoenix, tortoises, dragons, and other creatures. Parades are organized with dancing dragon and lion troupes. These dances were originally meant to scare away demons, but today they have become the symbol of the Chinese New Year celebrations.

DISCARD
THE
CURRENT
INSTANT